Endymion Awake

poems

Joseph Hart

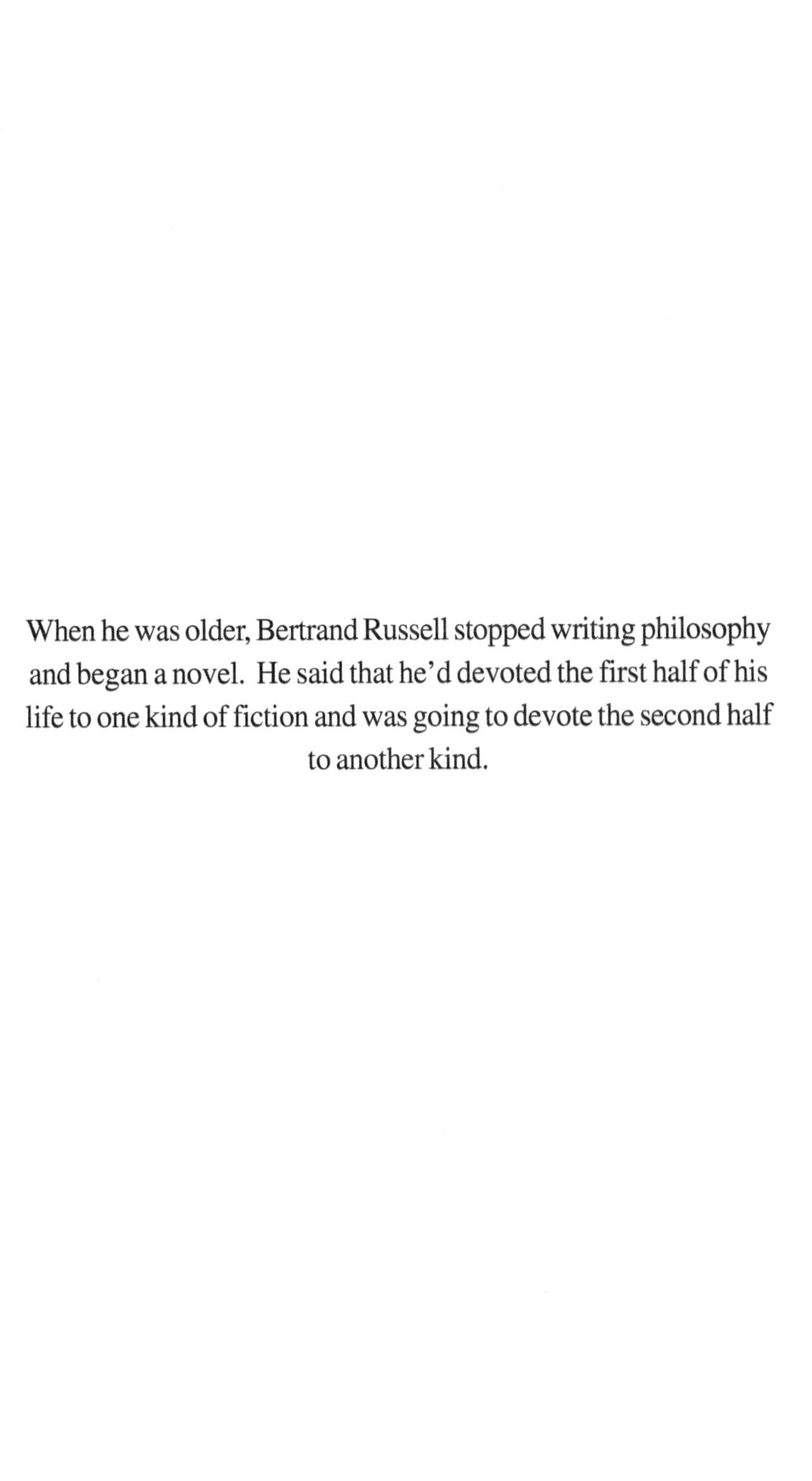

When he was older, Bertrand Russell stopped writing philosophy and began a novel. He said that he'd devoted the first half of his life to one kind of fiction and was going to devote the second half to another kind.

(dreamt poems)

Contents

Ragged Lines 9

Sensation 11

The Spell 12

Lines on the Ocean 13

To — who thought of it 14

The Castle 15

The Scene 17

The Ocean Remembered 18

A Foggy Night 19

A Sleep 21

A Rock Castle 22

The Fog 24

The Waves 25

The Soothing Sea 26

The Rose/The Sea 27

Fancy 28

Sleep 29

The Ocean and Sleep 30

The Storm 32

A Moment 34

Winter Wishes 35

A Winter Ocean 36

Depression 38

Lines on the Ocean and Sleep 39

Depths 40

A Picture on My Wall 41

The Bargain 42

Poems 43

Paradox 44

The Dreamer 45

Warm Feelings 46

The Fog 47

Seaside 48

Impressions 49

Belief 50

Other Lines 51

Feeling 52

Endymion Awake 53

The Old Sea 54

An Image 55

A Meadow 56

Rain 57

An Instance 58

The Beach 59

Ghosts 60

Intentions 61

Void 62

Nonentity 63

Verse 64

Paradox 65

Fantasy 66

Memory 67

Image 68

The Love Potion 69

Sensations 70

Loneliness 71

The Words 72

Weeping 73

Anachronos 74

Aphorisms 75

Romance 76

Imagination 77

Housman 78
Poe 79
Lines 80
The Mother 81

Ragged Lines

The castle's circular towers
Arise to the ceiling, the sky.
The ruined tombs and the blasted trees
Emit a silent cry.
And death will come
As some unsummoned calm
To soothe away
The grief and the regrets.
The sea will smooth the sand,
And like a balm,
An anodyne - the ocean quite forgets
That never did remember anyway.
Upon the sand, my subtle heart may find
A shell, a piece of coral
Or a stone
That eases or arouses in its kind.
To find a shell
Half-buried in the sand
And hold it snugly
In my sensive hand,
To feel its edges,
Look upon its color.
To dream about a phantom or a skull or
A ghost that wafts about the chilly gloom
In the sleepy corner
Of a dim archaic room
Musty, lighted by a candle-lamp.
The tapestries are faded,

Old and damp.
The castle's solid, stoic,
Heavy, old -
A dim medieval hymn exhales
With breath into the cold.
The castle stands upon a distant hill.
The air around it is so very still.
Its turrets rise but do not touch the sky.
Its ghosts are dead, so do not fear to die.
The stolid castle walls are very thick.
About the stout portcullis
The wind is cool and quick.

9-17-84

Sensation

The superannuation of the rocks
That craggy rise around the lucent waves
Bespeak an ancient ocean. Is a sleep
The succedaneum for such a sea?
Unutterable winds upon the surf
Uplift it into vapor on the sand.
And all that I can hear is what I dream;
And all that I can sense is what I feel.
The sky is like the surface of the sea,
All littered with the beds of little clouds.
And the ocean, like a warm and living hand,
Writes its perfect poems in the sand.
And there is no contradiction
In the presence of the sea.
And that sense should think of paradox
Is paradox to me.
Since all the earth is novel
And every life is new,
How can there be paradox
Or anything seem strange?
And the gentle oxymoron
Of the whisper of the sea
Leaves mercy in the infant
And leaves evening to me.

12-25-84

The Spell

My hollow heart is haunted
In the middle of the night.
I stand beneath the mystic moon
And feel a subtle fright.
A flock of birds is screaming wildly
In its distant flight.
A talisman, an ochre charm
Protects me from the sight.
The spell's a book. The book is Keats.
The magic is the verse.
His poetry's enough to ward
Away the darkling curse.
But in addition I have had
Two decades to rehearse
The sentiments and images
In his pentameter.
I hold at bay the midnight's sea
With this familiarity.

8-13-84

Lines on the Ocean

Upon a rock and kindredly
My senses feel and I can see
The sudden upshot of the sea
In strange familiarity,
All gentle in close harmony.
Relaxed, untense in present sense
My senses are my sentiments.
The air is salty, and the sea
Is grey and undulating free.
The farthest seagull overhead
Produces noises like the dead -
Those dead that occupy the graves
Of ocean suds and mindless waves.
The china sky is lightly blue,
But nothing in the sea is new.
Of all the songs that singers sing,
The ocean is the oldest thing.
But I am here and strangely free.
Yes, I am here. The sea! The sea!
I feel a union with the sea
But from a distant boulder.
Yes, I am here. The sea! The sea!

8-14-84

To — who thought of it

Come visit me, my olden love.
Renew and warmly make an
Acquaintanceship in current love
And gently reawaken
Those tender feelings in my heart
That I have not forsaken.
My love requires no design.
It simply can be taken.
The winter's gone and flowers bloom
Among the matted clover.
Come sit near me and do not say
That yesterday is over.
Be with me as you were, my love,
My ancient love the same.
And lay a flower on my stone
And sit beneath my name.

8-15-84

The Castle

I want to see a castle.
I want to feel the stone.
I want to sense its history
While feeling I'm alone.
I want to lean against the rock
And rough and rising walls,
To feel my shoulders on the hard,
Uneven surface there.
I want to wander with a ghost
Along some narrow halls
And sense the cold indifference
To warm and human prayer.
I want to touch a castle
All angular and square
And grey and rugged, hard and rough
With inner darkness dim,
To hear some Gothic singers chant
An old medieval hymn
And sense a whispered silence
In the dismal interim.
I want to pass a day and night
And relish every hour,
To climb the stairs irregular
And cramped into a tower,
And walk along the battlements
That overlook the sea,
To sense inside this castle made
Of rock inhuman, me,
A thing of warmth and consciousness

That I've identified
Inside this cold and cultured rock
Where god could not abide,
That hasn't any senses
Nor any love beside.
I want to touch a castle,
To seem to know its story
Archaic and outlasting me,
A hard memento mori,
Where ghosts not deities reside
And god himself's demystified.
I want to sense the history
All native to it mien,
To revel in the mystery
That I cannot explain.
I want to touch the surfaces
Of rough, uneven stone,
To wander in the courtyard
Unequivocally alone.
I want to feel the breath of wind
That whistles through the towers,
The same that centuries ago
Came rushing through the hours
That were so similar to mine
But happened long ago.
I want to see a castle,
Just to feel it, just to know
A castle there in England
When the mists begin to blow.

8-16-84

The Scene

Both plain and Gothic were the hills
Above the even shore;
The ocean waves exchanged themselves
In gentle evermore.
Ineffable the castle stood
Sequestered on the heath.
A low wind made the banners flap
Definable as breath.
A green and silver pond was near
The castle's rocky shore,
And in the distance made the sea
A solemn, sullen roar.
Upon the dismal plain the shrubs
Did grip the graveled ground.
Above it all the castle stood,
Imposing and misunderstood,
Within it all the castle stood
And made a silent sound.

8-16-84

The Ocean Remembered

Somehow I can imagine
Forevermore the sea
Albeit very long ago
And very far away.
I can remember rocks and shells
And endless drifting sand
As sensual and obvious
As looking at my hand
That is before me now.
I hear the sounds of flying gulls
That circle over swells
And smell the scent of seaweed
Stranded on the shore.
The sea has many spells
To cast upon an anguished heart.
A heart forevermore.
I see a dark and dismal sky
Above a cold and gloomy sea.
I'll never ask the ocean why.
Its deep geography
Is sleep enough for me.
And sleep's a sea, another sea
Whose currents grip the heart of me
And pull me down among the waves
Whose motions cross and counter-cross
But evermore serene.
Ah, sleep's a sea, another sea
Whose heart archaic waits for me.

8-25-84

A Foggy Night

The moon's a circle in the night,
The stormy night
Where clouds are thick and heavy
Above the sea, the singing sea
Whose voice is deep and low
A bass among the heavy swells
That shatter on the shore.
A sense of sleep pervades the mist
That circles o'er the sea,
And he is blind inside the fog
Who walks across the sand.
The fog is deep and wet and cold.
He feels it with his hand.
His fingers clench but cannot grip
The insubstantial ghost
Of damp and dismal fog whose clouds
Are passing through each other.
The ocean thunders in the fog
That quietens the sound.
The swells arise, then suddenly
Spread open on the sand,
Spread even on the sand,
A moment pause, then suddenly
Go out to sea again.
The moon's a candle in a lamp
Above the muffled sea.
The heaving soul, the breast of sand
Receives the subtle waves.
The moon's a candle in a lamp,

A circle overhead.
The cloudy moods of spectral fog
Have covered deep the shore.
The fog is like an ocean
With currents, swells and waves.
Like pallid smoke, it boils about,
Obscures the gravid sea.
Inside the fog there is a sense
Of sleep, of soothing sleep.
The ocean's self inhabits now
The castle of the fog.
The moon's a candle in a lamp,
A single ochre eye
That looks upon the book of fog
And listens to the sea.
The moon, a candle in a lantern
Gutters in the night
Where all is dark and wet with fog;
Yet I can hear the sea.
A single passerby alone
Among the shifting fog
Is leaving footprints in the sand.
The ocean will erase them.
The murky fog and darkling sea
Have touched the heart of him, and he
Has felt the heart of them.

8-28-84

A Sleep

What is god? And where is god?
And what is god to me?
So she dreamed of god yclept
While warmly she completely slept.
Gods are nonsense. Gods are myth.
The warmth that she was sleeping with
Was in the blankets round her throat.
Upon the sea of sleep, her boat
Was gently rocked by every wave.
Old sleep is like a conscious grave.
She yawned and turned while sleeping on
Until she reached the rock of dawn
On which she moored her little ship
Until she took another trip.
Forgotten gods are gods forgot.
The fingers of a sleep have not
A single god for dreaming of.
Love is sleep, and sleep is love.

8-31-84

A Rock Castle

The castle stands encrusted
In the open hands of rock
As if it were enfolded
In the petals of a flower.
And every day the subtle rain
Erodes the castle walls;
And when they are erased into
The dust of nothingness,
There will have been a castle
Once pronounced among the rocks.
The rocks are grey and angular
And harder than the rain;
But nonetheless the constant rain
Will weather them away.
Within the castle houses
Chilly anechoic rooms
Whose walls are rock and hard and cold,
Unsubtle to the touch.
Within the castle houses
The dimensions of the rooms
All empty, square and cold and grey
With earthy, grassy floors.
The castle is a remnant
From the history of sleep,
A sleep of history, a rock
Leviathan of dreams.
I seem to sense a sense of sleep
Imagining the walls;
The castle gives a swelling feel,

A depth and an excitement;
But it is old and rock and hard
And rough and angular.
I seem to sense a sense of sleep
From thinking of the stone.
Its graveled battlements are sleep;
The dream is quite alone.

8-29-84

The Fog

A mournful ululation through the fog
Summons up a dismal ghost of sleep.
The movement of the fog is most profound.
Its movement is serene and makes no sound.
It gently moves among the alleyways
And covers all the buildings that it passes.
A sleep's a ghost and moving through the fog.
The fog's a ghost.
The two ghosts meet and merge
Among the deep and darkened midnight air.
The fog is feathery. Its tongue
Goes out ahead of it
And licks the buildings that it will consume.
The fog is very soothing
To the sight of one who sees.
A grey, pulsating, undulating
Mist along the streets
Cool and moist and obfuscating, warm
Surrounds the people passing
With the density of sleep
And makes the buildings shadows in the darkness.

9-2-84

The Waves

I feel and with a deep recovery
The tender instauration of the sea
Revivify in depth the heart of me.
The ocean comes to my imagination.
I wonder what the waves are saying now.
The lazy waves create a calm sensation.
As if my body were a vessel's prow,
I dip below the surf and feel it lull
And lap the hollow shoulders of my hull.
I sit beside the restless soothing sea.
The ocean is another sleep to me.
The breakers rise and make a giant bow.
I wonder what the waves are saying now.
The surface of the surf is wet with foam.
And in my fantasy I'm going home
To be beside the ocean, cool and wet
Where I can be alone and quite forget
The fever in my temples and my brow.
I wonder what the waves are saying now.
I sit beside the ruins of the sea.
"Forget! Forget! Remember only me!"
And that is what the waves are saying now.
And that is what the waves are always saying.

The Soothing Sea

The sea, the sea, the soothing sea,
A deeply soothing ocean-sea
That understands the heart of me
Makes an obfuscating roar
Upon the underlying shore.
The ocean soothes my troubled heart.
The fog obscures completely
My senses and my common sense.
The sand is wet and crumbles
Beneath my feet beside the sea
That understands the heart of me.
Thalassic waves are soothing.
My naked feet upon the sand
In wave-made ridges gently stand.
I look upon the soothing hand -
The ocean on my forehead.
The motives of a single heart
Are easy to discover.
The ocean soothes a troubled soul
And loves a loveless lover.
The motives of a heart are nowhere
Deeper than the sea
Whose shallow, obfuscating roar
Makes them appear confusing.
The sea, the sea, the soothing sea
Relaxes hearts in vivo
And with its roll allows a soul
To understand - nothing.

9-2-84

The Rose/The Sea

A sense of déjà vu comes over me
As I kneel beside the rose beside the sea.
I think I've seen this subtle rose before
Beside an early ocean's ancient roar.
The soothing sea is giving me a sound
But doesn't wake the flower that I found.
Its gentle face is pink and rusty red.
I touch it the more gently with my hand.
It might have been while dreaming in my bed
That I saw this rose that's rooted in the sand.
The ocean's words possess the sense to heal.
And standing in an underset I feel
My body and my sense pulled either way.
(How serious are children in their play!)
The ocean nullifies the sense of doubt
And misery I feel. And round about
The hills of sand are shifting like a Sphinx.
The sea is soothing to a soul who thinks.
It touches an archaic depth in me
And fosters out familiarity.

Fancy

So why not let my fancy
Wander free?
I want to be a ghost
Awafting in the twilight
Who haunts a chilly sleep
In the corner of the sea.
I want to feel
The ocean beat the shore,
To be devoured
By its mighty roar.
I want to feel a truth
I never felt.
I want to be a phantom
Invisible and cool
And to haunt the earth forever
In a universal sleep;
To be a ghost
And sleep for aye
Awake forever
In a sweet unrest.

9-12-84

Sleep

I feel the shape of warm escape
Come over me like sleeping.
In want of pain the world is sane
When I am in a dream.
All hurt is gone into a yawn
And suddenly I'm sleeping.
Surreal bliss, a lover's kiss
Are privy to a dream.
And when I wake it seems to take
Some minutes to stop sleeping.
I keep the feel that it is real
What only was a dream.
I wish it were to reoccur
And I could go on sleeping.
On ocean sands I feel the hands
Of lovers in a dream.
The ocean's noise is counterpoise
In that event called sleeping.
A lover's hands make soft demands
When I am in a dream.
And even when a denizen
Of horror occupies it,
A sense of bliss, a subtle kiss
Surfeit the common dream.

9-9-84

The Ocean and Sleep

I rest upon the beach of sleep
And gaze into the sea.
The subtle wind is like a yawn
And washes over me.
The sand is warm, uneven and
The rocks are rough and hard
And steep. They catch the breakers
And make a stoic guard
Around the gentle cavern,
Beside the rhythmic seas.
The ocean is a flower.
I sleep in tender ease.
No fretful dream awakes me
Alone upon the shore.
The ocean makes a lullaby
With its own muffled roar.
It's sleep that muffles what I hear
And makes it far away
What really is quite close and near.
What do the sea waves say?
Fresh sleep interprets what they say
But do not say to me
And makes of them a changeling dream.
I sleep beside the sea.
The subtle, soothing ocean waves
Are nurturing and lull
My body into changing dreams
That occupy my skull.
And I dream about the ocean,

I dream about the sea,
I dream about a gentle wind
That washes over me.

9-12-84

The Storm

The ship's bell rings. And the sound
Echoes through the cotton fog
That muffles the sound.
A storm is due.
The moon's a ghost and sinks behind
The ghostly, spectral clouds.
A froth is on the ocean waves
That lunge forever larger.
The ship is lifted by a swell
And settles on the sea again.
Beneath the incipient storm
The fish swim in their ease.
The grey waves cradle the wet ship
And heave it on its side.
The sullen fog is rhythmless
And boils across the deck
In puffs of breath and giant clouds
All ghostly and serene.
The phantom fog
Is moist and hollow
And seems to move
Like giant sleep awake.
The thunder like a slamming door
Shatters the still gloom.
The lightning is a distant flame
Far out and deep at sea.
And then the rain!
It slants and drives
And thunders on the sails.

The mast is sticking through the mist
And tilts against the sea.
The rain is steady and unbroken
By the whole explosions
Of the thunder out at sea.
The lightning is a skeleton
Emblazoned on the mist.
The rain, the fog, the ocean
In a raging harmony
All surround
The wooden ship at sea.

9-12-84

A Moment

Beside the sea
The sunlit sea
Whose gloomy waves
Come over me,
I fall asleep,
To sleep profound
And hear the sea
Without a sound.
The clouds are lulling
In the sky.
I hear a lonesome
Seagull cry.
I sleep upon
The placid sand
Beside a rock.
My human hand
Forgets the sea,
Remembers sleep
That like the ocean
Is as deep.
The truth is that
There is no truth at all.
I hear a distant
Seagull's call.

9-13-84

Winter Wishes

I will be glad when winter comes,
The inner beating of warm drums,
The leafless trees, gaunt, cold and bare,
A frozen breath, a gloomy prayer.
I warmly wish again to pass
Through murky fog on icy grass,
To fondle flowers, red and blue
All withered to another hue.
Old winter is an empty hull
All hollow, beached, abandoned
(An infant playing with a skull)
Of an archaic galley.
I wish another winter here! -
A winter weather cold and drear
With several blankets on a bed.
In shallow, deep, delicious dread
I can go walking, found and lost
In coats and sweaters through a frost,
Or else imagine and indite
The subtle magic of the night.
Rainy, human, cold and right,
Reading Proust by candlelight.
I wish such weather wouldn't pass.
(Pigeons on the grass alas.)

8-8/9-84

A Winter Ocean

It pleases me when winter comes!
A foggy rain, a windy chill,
A somnolence I feel until
The winter wakes the heart of me
Beside an atavistic sea.
I wish the winter weather were
Upon the earth and I could stir
To walk through fog and feel the mist
Reflected in an amethyst.
A chilly kiss (but not from death)
That makes a sudden ghost of breath!
The sand is moist. The fog is deep.
I feel as if I were asleep
And that my heart had soft been kissed
While I was a somnambulist.
The lazy sea across the land
Leaves a trace upon the sand
Another wave erases
And leaves one trace the more
Across the shore.
Nook-shotten rocks all angular
Are nestled in an evening fog
In massive piles. A single star
Above the wintry seascape soars
And overlooks a hundred shores.
I feel this winter weather stir
A deep and sweet elation.
I see such weather as it were
In my imagination.

The soothing fog from off the sea
Becomes a ghost surrounding me.
Upon a boulder I shall sit
And feel the sea. Each subtle fit
Of waves across an empty shore
Satisfies my glad heart more.
And all the sea and all its sound
Discover what I never found -
A trace, a face, a commonplace.
The swift succeeding waves erase
Each wave and foot mark in the sand
As they expand.
Bless the sea, indifferent sea,
That makes my heart a memory!

9/84

Depression

Except for this thalassic rose
That grows beside the sea,
There's scarce the spectre of the sense
Of former revelry.
And now the shadows of the night
Are darkening the dawn,
And sleep must stay, nor go away:
A fog, a carillon.
The sleep that every night comes quick
At dawn is slowly spent.
The ostinato of the rain
Is like a cerement.

7-26-85

Lines on the Ocean and Sleep

The fragile ghosts
About the government of sleep
Waft among the rafters
While the castle-night is deep.
The sea's awash
Upon the everlasting beach.
Waves wet the darkling sand
As far as they can reach.
The night is dim
And spectral on the sea.
An interim of ocean
Fosters sleep's soft mystery.
The sea is deep,
But sleep that holds its own
Is deeper than the ocean.
And both of them I've known
Or felt and loved.
The narcoleptic sea
Sleeps upon the silent shore
In subtle poetry.

9-24-84

Depths

Excepting in the grave of sleep
(So deep as any ocean)
I can become more conscious
Everyday.
But have I ever slept so deeply
As my heart can go?
When my wishes are suppressed
My heart is an abandoned thing -
A ghost that treads the wind
As if in water -
A shape or form
That hasn't any color,
Any nuances or subtleties
Or love.
But dormant dreams
My ombudsmen
Investigate the matter.
And I awake with relics
And shadows of the dreams
Lurking in unfinished memory.
Sleepy dreams now occupy
My waking memory incomplete.
And old imagination
Is ever young for aye.

10-7-84

A Picture on My Wall

The gnarled, wind-wetted, wooden posts
Point blindly to the sea,
Stuck in the sand around the rocks
In rugged, old complaisance.
The seagulls crown the inner air
With swoops of flight and noises.
Their double crescents, grey and white,
Swim just above the swells.
The reef of rocks in silhouette
Rears ragged from the sea.
The taste of salt is in the sand.
The old posts slant and lean.
And all is blue and all is grey.
The ocean's deadly rustle
Washes up against the rocks
And then goes back to sea.
In the sky, the subtle clouds
Are like the puffs of breath
Against a hand when someone speaks.
The wind is cool and warm.

10-8-84

The Bargain

His narcoleptic trances
Were a voluntary thing
Because he loved to sleep,
He loved to dream.
And while awake his interest
Was thinking of his dreams
That went in wisps and subtleties
Throughout his memory.
So then he asked the god of death
To let his death come early
And in exchange for dying
Let him dream forevermore.
The god of death consented,
And he lay inside his tomb
Dreaming with a whole imagination

10-8-84

Poems

A poem should give pleasure.
That is all a verse is for.
But if it can with magic keys
Unlock a bolted door
And disclose a truth or paradox
That's psychological,
It with a sense of memory
Happily can lull
The heart to sleep of pleasant dreams -
And that is poetry.
A poem must come like a dream
With all the sense of sleep
And ought to please at bottommost,
A pleasure one can keep
At hand or in one's memory
Forever soft and new
And touch the heart and inner heart
On surface and at depth.

10-9-84

Paradox

My intelligence does not believe in god.
It sees the sham and fable of it all.
But nonetheless my feelings are devout
And love their god and dream of afterlife.
And both of them together wholly loathe
The Middle Ages, fundamentalists
Which make my feelings disbelieve in god,
As do the many horrors of the earth
To human life and other animals.
I think of these and suddenly I lose
My sleepy, dreamy, warm belief in god.

10-15-84

The Dreamer

Though sleep be like a mother's hand
The dreamer is alone
Who in his tender dream can feel
The ancient myths of Greece
As if he touched a string upon
An antiquated lyre
And summoned up another tune
From an archaic dream.

11-27-84

Warm Feelings

I sit alone and listen to the sea
Until its shadow washes over me
And feeling-senses are in reverie.
I gaze upon a flower til my eyes
Have ceased to see and their sensation dies,
And they are numb and cannot see to glance.
I whisper in the séance of a trance
And summon up the spectre of my soul.
When sleep's awake a ghost comes to my room
And conjures up a shadow in the gloom,
The spirit of a personal perfume.
The moon's alone. I cannot tell you how
I am alone and listen to the sea.
This cloudy moon is company enow.
And poetry is my identity.

12-4-84

The Fog

The fog drifts numbly past the door
And through the branches of the trees
Whose branches are the spectres
Of the night.
The fog has made a shadow
On the ground.
An interesting feeling this -
To wander through the misty fog
Invisible unto myself
As if I were a ghost.
When I am in the fog, I am
Inside a womb.
I am a ghost.
The fog itself - the mother ghost -
The mother ghost of all.

12-13-84

Seaside

Unkindness is a shallow thing,
But kindness is profound.
I sit upon the seaside
And listen to the sound
Of tumbling waves and breakers
That spread across the shore.
I could sit so forever -
At once, forevermore.
There is in my sensations
The subtle sense of sleep,
A feeling that I cherish
And wish for aye to keep.
An interesting feeling
So sitting by the sea
Comes over me in solitude.
And senses soft agree.

12-13-84

Impressions

Honesty is truth,
But kindness is profound.
And all about the ocean
There is mercy in the sound
Of waves that soothe the senses
And heal a troubled heart.
And the ocean recommences
When its frothy waves depart.
But the touch of sleep upon me
Puts sensation into rest,
Sensing sleep alone in dreams
I never could have guessed.
And a single seagull loiters
In the grey above a boulder.
In the shadow of the ocean
I am never getting older.
In the fog the sea is murky
Though a magic spell it weaves
With its sounds deep in the silence,
Like the falling of soft leaves.

12-25-84

Belief

Sudden on awakening
I still believed the dream
That my heart one minute past
Had in belief been dreaming.
And with a fable of my sense,
An image in my feelings
I concoct a fantasy
That nourishes my heart.
But such an image, such a thought
Or such a fantasy
Becomes in subtle fact the air
My wishes notwithstanding.
It's only when I am asleep
In fact or in effect
That warmly I can safely keep
My dreams uncontradicted.

7-30-84

Other Lines

I listen to a gull -
Whatever it believes -
And repose upon a boulder
Where the solemn ocean grieves.
And I listen to the whisper
Of the surf across the shore,
And I gaze toward the sky
And see the clouds and nothing more.
And the presence of the ocean
Is a thing of depth, as deep
As its feeling in my body,
Like the subtle sense of sleep.
As my eyesight softly falls
Upon the surface of the sea
All wholesome, without paradox
The paradox of me
Questions how can anything
Be supernatural
Since all that is is nature
However it may be,
So supernatural is only
Terminology.

12-26-84

Feeling

Beneath the winter skies
I sit upon a rock beside the sea
That presages my incipient demise
And gives a sense of immortality.
And by the sea I have been kissed,
Upon my body, so my soul.
I feel cold bubbles in the mist
And listen to the shoal.

1-1-85

Endymion Awake

Today I think I choose to do
What I have done unthinkingly.
I'm conscious of the love
And what I love.
Once I was somnambulist.
Then I was asleep.
And now I am awake and want to do
The things that in my sleep I dreamt I did.

1-5-85

The Old Sea

To fall asleep beside the sea
Is like a double bliss
Where in my sense the sea and sleep
Meet gently in a kiss.
But the mournful ululations of the sea
Sound like an ancient soul in jeopardy.
Deep-sunk, the rocks are buried in the shore
Impervious to ocean, wind and roar.
And now a fog is coming from the sea.
It hides the shore from all, and all from me.
Nonetheless the ocean happily
Continues its archaic rhapsody.
I feel a sense of oldness
In thinking of the sea.
It's heavy in my stomach
And my chest. The heart of me
Is like a string the ocean
Plays its elder tunes upon
That echo in the memory
When present sense is gone.
My feelings are the stuff on which
The sea leaves its impression.
And I feel some mesmerism
By the waves in their succession.

1-6-85

An Image

The subtle consternation of the sea,
The constant sea that sleepily engulfs
The sodden, deep-sunk posts of wooden piers
Is heaving its involvements to the sand.
The sky is low. Already I can feel
The nearness in an image
Of the deepness of the sea.
I see the sea in human conjuration.
Up from my depth I think the depth
Of oceans.
About the sea - I wonder what there is
About the sea; a magic I can touch
About the sea.

1-7-85

A Meadow

I see a summer meadow sweet with gold
Swaying in a free, thalassic breeze
That's salty with the scent of ocean spray.
I see two birds sink slowly in the sky
And rise again, descend, as if they were
The shadows of two branches in a breeze.
To sit upon a stone and see the sky -
A whisper overhead, the sky appears
As happy as a baby's nascent smile
Without a mist, where random bits of clouds
Like cotton ragged-torn from bigger hunks
Without direction wander on the blue.

1-8-85

Rain

I see the moisture of the rain
Falling on the window pane,
And in my sense I see the sky.
Unfettered clouds are floating by.
Deep and low the thunder wells.
A sudden gust of wind expels.
The air is cold. The room is damp.
A wind extinguishes the lamp.
I see the image of a chair,
A darker shape in darkness there.
I hear the raindrops overhead.
I feel the softness of the bed.
The walls seem distant and serene
In darkness. What does darkness mean?
The darkness in the room is clear,
Heavy, dense and is no pall.
And I have fantasized it all.
Are darkness, wind and rain sincere?

1-10-85

An Instance

Why do I remember this?
I've done for many years.
Because of what it means?
For how it feels?
For both? Or for another
Reason altogether?
But nonetheless I savor what
I do not understand,
And I love it,
Though I can not tell you why.

1-11-85

The Beach

And all that I can feel is what I sense
While I wander near the ocean
Where the waters recommence
Their regular sensations.
With the fingers of my hand
I can dig into the moisture
Of the grainy, crumbling sand,
Transient, eternal,
Overturn the broken shells,
Unbury and dislodge them
With my naked feet and toes,
Look and listen to the swells
While the nascent twilight grows
Inchoate and becoming.
This is memory and deep,
As soothing as a whisper.
This is pleasure. This is sleep.

1-19-85

Ghosts

I can believe in ghosts
Until I think of what I feel.
A ghost inconsequential
Isn't altogether real.
To be nothing but a noise
On the other side of walls -
A dream itself is dreaming
Where the evening's shadow falls -
To waft about a rafter
In the ceiling overhead -
As living as the ocean,
But as dead -
To be as dead.

2-2-85

Intentions

When I was young
(Or rather old)
A poet known as Keats
Was both my best companion and my friend
Probably for 20 years or so.
And notwithstanding my design
To write some perfect poems
(Perfectly imperfect)
I felt another wish more singular:
To write a book of poems
That another heart would read
In ancient time to come
And feel as warm and understood
As I had felt from Keats.
In contradiction never did
I want my poems published.

2-23-85

Void

I don't want my poems published.
I was thinking yesternight
While I slowly fell asleep
Of destroying all my poems,
Chucking every one of them.
And in consequence I felt
I was a void among the objects,
An emptiness imagined
That was nearly tangible.
Though not of plain indifference
I apperceived a state
Of nothingness, not mattering,
A vertigo of grief,
But in an image of despair
As if I had no nature
But the things I was aware of,
No body but a consciousness of pain:
The pain of nothingness.
As if I had no person whatsoever.

2-27-85

Nonentity

It is not the great emotions
Understandable to all,
It is just the little feelings
I cannot articulate
(The passing pains, impossibilities,
The cold misunderstandings)
That like rivulets create
A silent sea of pain
Subterranean and deep
That I never could communicate,
Explain except with death.
And oftentimes it seems
That were it not for agony
I would not be alive.
It is just the little feelings
I cannot articulate.

2-27-85

Verse

The sea is moving in its sleep.
A pulse of thundercloud
Gluts the evening sky.
And evermore is everywhere.
A breeze is breathing in the air.
A shallow mist to hide despair
Encourages the sea.

2-27-85

Paradox

I imagine the ocean -
An image within -
But I nevertheless
Feel the sea on my skin.

3-5-85

Fantasy

Sitting in my room of rock,
Rock-supported walls,
I'm free to dream of anything at all
Since some of it will seem to be
(Therein its interest)
And none of it be true.
And when I die
The dream will be extinguished,
Though the chamber will endure,
But even it will perish one fine day,
As will the day.

3-1-85

Memory

I remember what was said to me
Thirty years ago
As if the words were uttered
Just today,
As if the one who said them
Still remembered what he said,
As if the speaker
Hadn't gotten old.

3-2-85

Image

Come soothe me, sea
And ease the pain.
No exit: no compassion.
Encourage me
To fall asleep
In my imagination.
I'll conjure up
A sensuous
Agreeable and lucid
Sightless image
Of blind sleep
That soothes me
Like the sea.

3-3-85

The Love Potion

I was in love with Melanie
But she did not love me.
I languished in despair
For want of her.
I needed an elixir
And I got it from a hag
Who promised that the potion
Would enamor her of me.
But I was too conceited
To effect a love like this.
Her love would not be voluntary.
It would be a spell.
So I said goodbye to Melanie.
She did not speak to me.
I'll drink the drug
And look into a glass.

3-3-85

Sensations

Must all sensations pass?
And is sensation like a structure,
A skeleton in which my soul belongs?
And could my heart as well be put
In any other body,
Sleepily imprisoned
In sensations not my own?

3-4-85

Loneliness

When we were together
I felt terribly alone.
Such sentiments
I'd never felt before.
And when we separated
I felt natural again.
In holding you
I seemed to hold a ghost.

3-7-85

The Words

The sounds of the words
That I dream in a dream
Seem enchanted and distant
And magical things,
Close and remote
And sincere, like the sea.
Can sleep be an idiom?
Or shall I see
Each particular literally?
Like a ghost in a garret
That dwells for an hour
And leaves in the sofa and chairs
Its scent, its aroma, its smell.

3-25-85

Weeping

Can I cry in an explosion
Like the painting by Picasso?
All my inner self feels swollen,
And my heart's already there.
To remember,
To imagine,
To see nothing:
But to cry.
In such painful, sweet exhaustion
I can feel deliverance.
It's a pleasant, tired evening.
Soon I'll be asleep.

3-25-85

Anachronos

All sensations pass,
And so do gods.
A sacred book unread
Will be forgotten
And all its verities
Exist no more.
But sleep will fill the gaps of time
And dinosaurs reborn
May thunder like a mountain on the earth
Or bellow like an ocean in the trees.

3-26-85

Aphorisms

What does life make?
Nothing except sense.
And god is only
An experience.
This god so grand, so awesome,
Historic and sublime,
This god is just a feeling
And it will pass in time.
To hear them talk
It seems forsooth
That most of all
God hates the truth.
As every feeling passes,
Diminishes, grows dim,
So would the sense of god
If I encountered him.

Romance

To stand upon a mountain
In the center of a storm
Inditing mighty poems to the rain,
Capturing the thunder,
Exhaling in the wind,
The page illumined by the lightning's glare!
To see the heavy boulders
Sunk in the pinnacle
And revel in the darkness everywhere!
To conjure up the phantom
Of a black and awesome cloud,
To sigh a human, unimmortal prayer!
To sense the very emptiness
Of sky that's not a thing
But darkness, feel the shadow of my soul!
To savor the excitement
Of so sublime a storm,
Look down and see the ocean ever roll!
There's not a haven anywhere
For even just a ghost.
And the storm is sleep itself that has exploded!

1968/1985

Imagination

Like waking from the perfect sense of dreams
To find them incoherent in the day,
So poems are a warm, imagined thing.
And when the spell is broken
The enchantment goes away.
To disengage my mind from everyday
And write a wealth of phantom poetry!
Nor are my verses altogether
Empty and unreal.
I feel the thoughts I write,
I just don't write the thoughts I feel.
It's a very easy thing to think in verse.
Not everything so thought makes poetry.
And my poems are original
Despite my love for Keats.
They are the breath of
My unconscious
And imagined heart.
Nor is living of more substance
Than imagination is.
Ah but is the psyche beautiful per se? -
Remembrances, sensations, feelings, thoughts?
In fantasized sensations I just say
The imagination of a pretty thing,
And conjure up my own profundities.
That's all I want my poetry to be.

1/85

Housman

Perfect little rhymes
That stud the end of lines -
Phrases of sad music
Like diamonds out of mines -

Not every song is sad
(An elegy for death) -
Though every song is beautiful -
And warm like living breath -

Very gentle beauty
And love in each refrain -
Is there genius in a poem? -
Is the beautiful humane?

Poe

A moody poet – Poe -
The feeling in his verse
Radiates the glow
Of someone in a hearse.

Little turns of thought,
At images adept
And melancholy love
With sadness from a crypt -

But less of this than madness,
Sorrowful and sad
And gloomy as a tale
Told by someone mad.

What became of Poe?
Beaten in an alley.
God only gave him tragedy
And love that's melancholy.

Lines

It takes a certain genius
To make a poem sing.
Keats, Millay and Housman
Are a few.
And it is a silly madness
To ask God for anything -
Although the helpless
And the hopeless do.

The Mother

His mother was old,
Mindless and sad -
The only mother
He ever had.

An odd Pieta -
Not blessed but grim -
She looked at her son.
Was she looking at him?

In the arms of his mother -
His mother was good -
His strength – and someone
Who understood.